The Way of the Cross
The Women of Jerusalem Follow Jesus

Marie Rouanet

Translated by
Linda M. Maloney

THE LITURGICAL PRESS
Collegeville, Minnesota

www.litpress.org

Cover design by Ann Blattner. Cover: "Procession of the Mysteries," Trapani, 1986. Photo © Franco Zecchin.

Translated from the French of *Chemin de Croix des Femmes de Jérusalem suivant Jésus dans sa Passion* (Paris: Desclée de Brouwer, 1999). Biblical citations in the original from the translation by Sr. Jeanne d'Arc, *Les Evangiles. Les quatre* (Paris: Desclée de Brouwer, 1992). English citations by the translator, adapted from the *New Revised Standard Version*.

1	2	3	4	5	6	7	8

Library of Congress Cataloging-in-Publication Data

Rouanet, Marie.
    [Chemin de croix des femmes de Jerusalem suivant Jesus dans su passion. English]
    The way of the cross : the women of Jerusalem follow Jesus / Marie Rouanet ; translated by Linda M. Maloney.
        p. cm.
    ISBN 0-8146-2710-2 (alk. paper)
    1. Stations of the Cross. I. Title.

BX2040.C4413 2001
232.96—dc21   00-052060

The Way of the Cross

Preface

I am not one of those people who make candelabra out of ox yokes or hat stands out of stags' feet; I am the type who will always regret that the Carthusian house at Villeneuve-lès-Avignon has become the cultural center we now know. Nothing makes me more melancholy than an object or a building diverted from its real function.

A long time ago, when I began to make regular visits to the house where I mostly live nowadays—my husband's family home—the abbey of Sylvanès was like one of those churches that are only occasionally opened. Everything about it felt abandoned. The abbey church was glacially cold and green with dampness at all seasons. What remained of the ancient walls, the cloister, the chapter house, were being used by a farmer. The scriptorium had become a sheep pen. There was a certain charm in finding that indestructible chamber filled with ewes and iridescent swallows that brushed against the visitor. The smell of manure, the bleating, the lanolin on the rows of columns rising toward the vaulted ceiling like lilies—that, at least, was life. It was less depressing than the all-but-dead church.

I have seen places of worship all over the place becoming tourist sites. In *Bréviaire* I wrote about a state

5

dinner held in a Cistercian abbey in Languedoc; it was utterly depressing. I told about the round tables and the roses occupying the nave, the "techno" ball in the chapter house. All the guests were gorging themselves, and I concluded my account bitterly: "The Cistercians lived in silence, were vegetarians, and sang Gregorian chant." I told myself that one of these days the Department or the Region would take a fatal interest in Sylvanès, and that something equally terrible would happen to it.

But something was watching over that shadowy valley circled by mountains shrouded in black forests, where, on emerging from the valley of the Sorgues, one quite suddenly beholds the unpretentious church perched, in a silence filled with echoes, like a great stone bird with outstretched wings. Sylvanès, my neighbor, had the good fortune to find not merely a manager, but a priest who was monk and prior in one: André Gouzes, a Dominican. Smoothing and polishing the stones, re-building, cleaning and putting things in order: those things are the business of artisans. Restoring the soul: that is the business of faith. What illuminates the abbey today is in the category of the imponderable. It is inhabited by grace. Understand me: the grace I am speaking of is the grace of faithful people at prayer. God is not automatically present in an architectural construction, no matter how admirable; God is present where a few people "gather in God's name." When I enter the church I sense that prayer more than the beauty of the vessel that contains it. I remember a chapel where, at any hour of the day, people would gather before a particularly ugly statue of Saint Rita, even though right beside it there were precious and beautiful statues "in the class of historic monuments." Isn't it faith above all that matters? At Sylvanès, during the Paschal vigil, I put greater value on the pile of wood prepared by the faithful for igniting the new fire, the springtide decoration with white hawthorn picked on the surrounding hills, the cloth on the communion table, its whiteness and its folds showing that hands have washed and ironed it—I put more value on those things than on the beauty of the vaulting.

Since I have been living permanently in my hill house I have followed the whole course of Holy Week at Sylvanès, from Tenebrae to the morning of the Easter light. I think I feared the Way of the Cross and the veneration of the cross most. The roots of that fear lay far back in childhood, when I saw the nuns weeping while I myself, despite all my efforts, was unable to shed a single tear. Mine was a religion of joy. Anything that smacked of pleasure in suffering revolted me. That is not too strong a word. I found a cheerful and athletic aspect in penance and mortification, something not at all sad, because in that way I would attain to God and eternal life. When someone invoked the martyrs, I saw angels, miracles, the crowns prepared for them, and never their gouged-out eyes or severed heads.

For a long time I had the same feeling about the death of Christ. I couldn't help experiencing it in light of Easter morning, the rebirth of vegetation, the new sun, the music of the bells.

That is why I would never have imagined myself writing a Way of the Cross. A "genesis," sure; an ascent of Golgotha, no. And yet, when André Gouzes asked me, on Good Friday of 1996, "Will you write a Way of the Cross for us soon?" I immediately accepted.

Why? I would have found it impossible to say. I seem to see a relationship between that acceptance and the penitential rite when my neighbor helped me to stand up by saying, "Arise, Marie, your deliverance is at hand." It seems to me that there is a link, even if it is not clear or evident.

In this Way of the Cross I have not tried to put myself in the place of the women of Jerusalem so as to make a historical reconstruction of their state of mind. This is a meditation on today. I am the one following the procession that brings to his torture this marginal one among the marginalized. It is I who look on, who weep, whom Jesus addresses. It is I who see my son going to his death, who understand better and sooner than the men the meaning of that wound opened in the female genitals that has engendered the life ultimately delivered up to death. It is I myself whom I judge when I show the women saying: "it is not we, it is they," another way of washing one's hands; in the process of harshly criticizing Mary Magdalene in the name of their good consciences as honest women. It is myself of whom I speak when I tell of their invasive maternal love. And it is everyone whom I invite to the procession when I speak of their aid given to the dying, the dead, the wounded, of all the vital tasks that are theirs: washing, weaving, feeding, running, remembering; and when I affirm their unshakeable confidence in the force of life, which perhaps is the other name for faith.

Marie Rouanet

1

Matthew 27:28-31

The soldiers stripped Jesus
    and clothed him with a scarlet robe.
They plaited a crown of thorns,
    and put it on his head,
    and a reed in his right hand.
They fell on their knees before him,
    mocking him, saying:
    "Hail, King of the Jews!"
They spat on him.
They took the reed and struck him on the head.
After mocking him,
    they removed the robe
    and put his own garments on him.

They condemned him. They did it. Not us. We don't make the laws. We know nothing about the justice of them, nothing but these fetid prisons, these public tortures, the cross on that hill, where the condemned suffer.

They condemned him for the very things we heard: the light of the Father, an intangible kingliness, a temple not of stones, but of words.

This royal mantel of derision, this anti-crown, this scepter made of one of those reeds that are called distaffs: all the things they found—they, not us—before the real ascent of sorrow begins: is this really none of our business?

Antiphon: *We are not responsible; our hands are clean of the shedding of any blood—can we really still believe that we are innocent?*

2

Matthew 26:55-56

At that hour Jesus said to the crowds:
 "Here you come with swords and clubs to seize me
 as though I were a bandit!
 Day after day I sat in the Temple, teaching,
 and you did not lay hands on me."
All that happened
 to fulfill the scriptures of the prophets.
Then the disciples, all of them,
 left him and fled.

He is laden with a cross: he, the gentle man, the one who welcomed our children to his evening bivouac under the trees, told them enigmatic stories, stories that chilled our hearts or made them glow like fire.

He was a human being, and not a human being—he did not strike, did not judge—a human being and more than a human being—one had only to touch the fringe of his robe.

In him there shone the picture of a child preaching in the Temple; women at the well passed along the glowing memory of him.

Antiphon: *In this man bearing his gibbet we see the child preaching in the Temple, the child whose luminous memory was handed on by women at the well.*

3

Mark 15:21-22

They forced a passer-by, Simon of Cyrene,
    who was coming from the field,
    —the father of Alexander and Rufus—
    to carry his cross.
So they brought him to the place called Golgotha.

When they fell, in the past, in a past so distant that it is outside of time, our arms received our children, cradled them, made of our arms a secure shell. Then we gave them a drink of fresh water and repaired their torn clothes.

We did not understand, then, what the old women said: that's all roses, charming concerns, honeyed anxieties. Even the pain of childbirth they called "the pretty sickness."

The time would come when nothing could be fixed, either with tenderness or with needles and fresh water.

What shall we say when our hearts are bursting?

Antiphon: *Their childhood falls are rosy, just honeyed anxieties.*
    When nothing can be soothed by tenderness and fresh water any more, what shall we say when our hearts are bursting?

4

John 19:25-27

Standing near the cross of Jesus were
   his mother
   and his mother's sister,
   Mary of Clopas,
   and Mary Magdalene.
Seeing his mother
   and, close beside her, the disciple he loved,
Jesus said to his mother:
   "Woman, here is your son."
Then he said to the disciple:
   "Here is your mother."
From that hour the disciple took her into his own home.

They stop in front of his mother. She is there, faithful like little John. She is silent. It was never any use talking to him, to ask for a reason, or for miracles: "My child, why have you done this to us?" "Look, they have no wine."

She had the total confidence of mothers and their demands on behalf of anguish as vast as their love.

His response was to place between her and him a blade that sliced, terribly, through the flesh. After that, she was silent. It was enough that she be there, present when necessary, absent when necessary. Silently. Anyway, is there any place for speech in the final desert?

It is all too complicated for her. First he changed from a child into a man; as a man he became Lord, and at this moment he is less than a child.

He moves his lips, parched with thirst and sorrow; on her is read more than can be heard: "Here is your son."

Antiphon: *He changed from a child into a man, from a man into Lord and master.*

He placed between her and him a blade that cuts the flesh to the quick.

How can she understand? At this moment he is again less than a child.

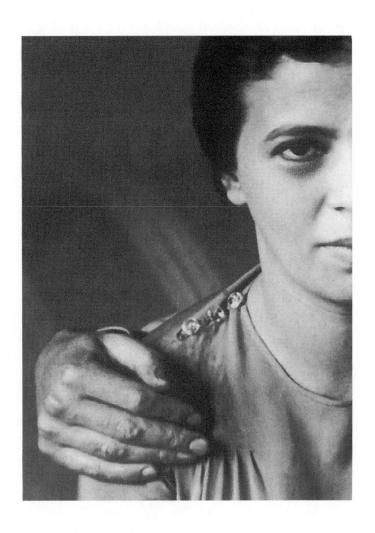

5

Mark 14:70-72

The bystanders said to Peter:
"Certainly you are one of them,
for you are a Galilean!"
He began to curse and swear:
"I do not know the man you are talking about!"
At that moment the cock crowed a second time.
Then Peter remembered
what Jesus had said to him:
"Before the cock crows twice,
you will have denied me three times."

The soldiers had to ask a stranger to help him. Not even a rubbernecker, not even a curious bystander: he was coming back from his field.

Of his own friends there is none left but the fair-haired boy, hardly more than an adolescent. The others? fled, hiding, cowards.

It's funny how we fear death after we are old. We see plenty of people die: being close to the dying is just part of women's work. Young mothers, hemorrhaging or eaten up with fever, often wait serenely, with open eyes. But old men and women scream out their anguish, gripping our hands, refusing to let go of life. Youth doesn't hang on so roughly. John is there: what does he care if someone recognizes him, and kills him tomorrow? Nothing matters to him except love.

How different it is with old Peter: before, he was always ready to talk and talk, to say "I love you," to protest his great attachment. First he says he's not one of their party; now he's gone. He was afraid for his ancient carcass. The so-called faithful have all fled. A stranger has to relieve him of the weight of the wood. Where it weighed on him, his garment is torn; from the shattered fruit of his shoulder the blood pours down: this is the human measure of fidelity.

Antiphon: *His garment is torn, his shoulder is a shattered fruit, his blood flows: this is the human measure of fidelity.*

6

Matthew 25:34-36

Then the king will say to those on his right:
   "Come, you blessed of my Father,
   inherit the realm prepared for you
   from the foundation of the world.
   For I was hungry, and you gave me food,
   I was thirsty, and you gave me drink,
   naked, and you clothed me,
   sick, and you visited me;
   I was in prison, and you came to me."

Everybody knew Veronica: always ready to help any cripple—human or animal—to bathe an old man filthy with excrement, to wash the dead, the ones who, without her, would have had to go without. We were not surprised to see her approaching Jesus, all beaten and wounded. She sponges, she wipes. The tenderness of her gesture is as important as the service itself.

Now her towel is soiled, as at the moment when we kill the lamb: with vivid red blood mixed with mucus.

It is we who usually do the washing, who, by great effort, make the dross of life vanish in the clear water.

But this is something else. We pass the rag from hand to hand, not knowing what it means: what of pity or pride, that we have been chosen, in our task as spinners, to receive this very first sign.

Antiphon: *Her towel is soiled with blood and mucus. We pass it from hand to hand. On this our work, our weaving, is inscribed the very first sign.*

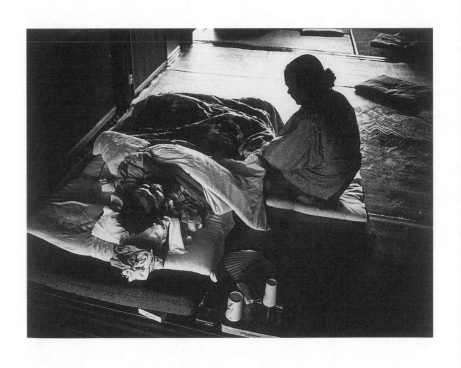

7

John 16:21-22

When a woman is in labor, she suffers,
    because her hour has come.
When the baby is born,
    she forgets her suffering because of her joy:
    a new human being has been born into the world.
And you are sorrowful now.
But afterward I will see you
    and your heart will rejoice
    and your joy no one will be able to take from you.

His mother keeps to the side of the road. Her eyes never leave him. She takes one step after another along with him. When he falls, she kneels. She is of earth, like us, bound to the joys and sorrows of living.

John, who supports her, is not earthy. He is illuminated from within, borne up by his flame: enamored. He has that air of exaltation that made people call him crazy. He doesn't care if they laugh at him when he sets his bare feet in the marks of his bare feet, smiling at the angels all the while.

At the moment when Jesus stumbles, we, like his mother, would love to see through John's eyes, to be able to look beyond the suffering and death of the Master.

Antiphon: *We are earthy, bound to the joys and sorrows of living. How we would like to see beyond the suffering and death of the Master.*

8

Luke 23:27-28

A great crowd of people followed him,
    among them women who were sobbing and lamenting
    for him.
Jesus turns to them and says:
    "Daughters of Jerusalem,
    do not weep for me.
    Weep instead for yourselves, and for your children!"

When Jesus told the men: "Let the one among you who has never sinned cast the first stone at her," they turned away. It was lucky he didn't say that to the women of Jerusalem: that adulterous woman would have been well and thoroughly stoned. We are so sure of being beyond reproach.

We should weep, as he asks us to, because we think we are without fault if our houses are in order, our deportment good, our linen clean, our accounts in balance.

Our men, in their violence and their consciousness of their own imperfection, may be better than we. Jesus, when you spoke to them, you were sure of saving that woman.

Let us weep. Many have abandoned you, and they all wanted to, when you lifted up the one we had judged so severely, puffing ourselves up over our own virtue. Let us weep. We did not understand at all that you turned the world upside down when you welcomed Mary Magdalene, that shameless painted wastrel—is there any place for perfume in our economy?—when you affirmed that to listen with open mouth and idle hands is the better part.

You have turned our souls inside out like socks, and we are afraid of that.

Let us weep, for we have turned aside from what is more difficult, saying: "He has no need of us; he prefers the do-nothings and the whores."

Antiphon: *Let us weep as he invites us to, for we have understood nothing. He has turned the world upside down; he has turned our souls inside out. Let us weep, for we have turned aside from the more difficult thing.*

9

Matthew 11:28-29

"Come to me,
    all you that are weary,
    all who are heavily laden,
    and I will give you rest.
Take my yoke upon you,
    and learn of me,
      for I am gentle and humble in heart."

Who will lift him up, beneath the blows of the guards' cudgels?

He will be above ground but a moment, hoisted on the cross.

He seems to us to recall how he lifted up those who were on the ground: the down-and-out, the sinners, the sick, even the dead. He was the one who lifted them up and gave them, with dignity, their true beauty in the light of love.

He, fallen three times, is without hope that someone in that crowd might stand up against injustice.

He can no more. One begins to wish that it could all be finished quickly.

Antiphon: *He lifted up those who were down and out.*
He was the one who raised them.
   In the light of love, he gave dignity and beauty.

10

And when they came to the place that is called The Skull,
they crucified him,
    with the criminals, one on his right and one on his left.
Jesus said:
    "Father, forgive them,
    for they do not know what they are doing."
They divided his garments
    by casting lots for them.

We have been virtuous and proud of being within the armor of our modest, brave, untiring garments, our mouths ever ready to slander and to scorn those we judge unworthy.

And then he came.

He was not one of those men who make the women keep quiet and stay in their place. But he looked at us, he made a gesture, spoke a word, and all at once we discovered that our hearts were dry. We were naked, without merit, equal to those we judged most harshly, equal among ourselves in his eyes, which pierced through appearances and went straight to the heart.

These garments the guards are dividing by lot: they seem to tell us that the Father is awaiting us this way, stripped, and that one day we will be able to offer Love nothing but love.

Antiphon: *He spoke a word and we discovered ourselves naked, with dry hearts.*

One day, stripped, we will be able to offer Love nothing but love.

11

John 19:32-34

Then the soldiers came:
they broke the legs of the first,
    then of the other who had been crucified with him.
Coming to Jesus, they saw that he was already dead,
    so they did not break his legs.
But one of the soldiers pierced his side with a lance,
    and immediately blood and water came out.

We followed. We stayed there, behind the line of soldiers, but we saw everything, heard everything: his thirst, his fear, his tenderness toward John and his mother, and also his pity for those more miserable than himself. We saw the collapsing of his body, to the last moment.

This blow of the lance that pierces him, this slit from which issue blood and water mixed, is like a woman's genitals, open and wounded; we know that it proclaims a birth.

Night has fallen on this gaping wound, now so peaceful. We open our eyes on the silent darkness.

And we await the arrival of the new child.

Antiphon: *Night has fallen on this gaping wound, now so peaceful. We await the arrival of the new child.*

12

Matthew 27:50-53, 55-56

Jesus again cried out with a loud voice
and gave up his spirit.
And behold: the curtain of the sanctuary
was torn in two, from top to bottom.
The earth shook.
The rocks were rent.
The tombs opened,
and many bodies of the saints who had fallen asleep
were raised.
After his resurrection they came out of the tombs.
. . .
Many women were there,
looking on from a distance.
They had followed Jesus from Galilee
and served him.
Among them were Mary Magdalene,
Mary the mother of James and Joseph,
and the mother of the sons of Zebedee.

The earth shook. We recognized the spasms of a contracting womb. These violently shaken clouds: see, they are like the faces of women at the moment of giving birth, sweating and twisted, but expressing something more than suffering.

We are the only ones who are not afraid; we even hide a ghost of a smile under our veils.

For from now on we will no longer give life on the threshold of mortal darkness, but in the hope of a life forever shielded from death.

The sky is red. The earth and all of us are born in that instant.

Antiphon: *The sky is red. From now on we will no longer give life on the threshold of mortal darkness.*

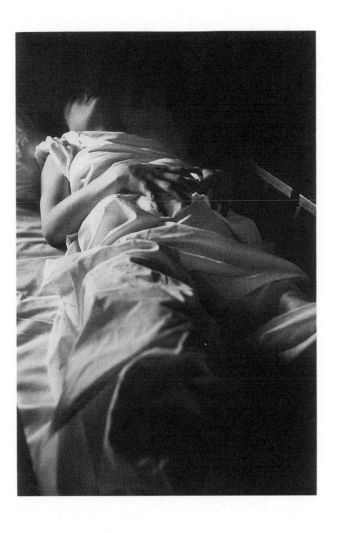

13

Matthew 27:57-61

When it was evening,
a rich man from Arimathea, named Joseph, came.
   He had also been a disciple of Jesus.
He went to Pilate
   and asked for the body of Jesus.
Pilate ordered it to be given to him.
Joseph took the body
   and wrapped it in a clean cloth.
He put it in a new tomb
   cut in the rock.
He rolled a great stone before the door of the tomb,
   and went away.
Mary Magdalene and the other Mary
   were sitting outside the tomb. . . .

E very mother bears, invisible, on her knees, and contemplates with fear a child with a human face, dead
to her and born to another, or to a god.

Antiphon: *Every mother bears, invisible, on her knees,
and contemplates with fear a child with a human face,
dead to her and born to another, or to a god.*

14

Luke 23:55-56

They followed closely, the women,
    the ones who had come with him from Galilee:
they saw the tomb
    and how his body was laid.
They went back
    and prepared spices and perfumes.
On the sabbath they rested
    according to the commandment.

We do the things necessary, troubling as little as possible the immobility of the heavens and the earth.

We prepare the body, comfort the mother and friends, make sure that they have enough to eat; we busy ourselves, keeping our mouths shut, almost. The world of women is full of silences, both good and bad: silence as sweet as the sleep of adults or of children well fed and protected by our vigilant weakness; the indescribable silence of the flesh and the heart in the face of death; the silence imposed on us; the silence that is prudent politics.

But we whisper what we have learned in the company of women: in the washhouse, at the oven, in the marketplace. We collect the memories of him, we store them up, we repeat them with tears so as never to forget them.

We are the first Gospel of all. It is he whom the wild nightingale recalls and sings in the icy night, in the light of a glowing fire, today and for all ages of ages.

Antiphon: *What does the wild nightingale sing except the first gospel of the women, the sheaf of memories gleaned at the oven, in the washhouse, in the marketplace?*
   What will the nightingale sing when it awakes, in the night illumined by a glowing fire, now and for all ages of ages? Amen.

Photo Credits